SELF-LOVE JOURNAL FOR TEEN GIRLS

SELF-LOVE JOURNAL FOR TEEN GIRLS

PROMPTS AND PRACTICES TO INSPIRE CONFIDENCE AND CELEBRATE YOU

CINDY WHITEHEAD

ROCKRIDGE PRESS

I'd like to dedicate this book to every young person out there who goes after what she/he/they wants and lives an authentic life.

Interior and Cover Designer: Elizabeth Zuhl
Art Producer: Sara Feinstein
Editor: Alyson Penn
Production Editor: Ellina Litmanovich
Production Manager: Holly Haydash

Illustration used under license from Shutterstock.com.
Author photo courtesy of Ian Logan.

Paperback ISBN: 978-1-63807-386-4
R0

THIS JOURNAL BELONGS TO:

_____

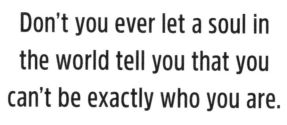

Don't you ever let a soul in the world tell you that you can't be exactly who you are.

—LADY GAGA,

actress, songwriter, and singer

SELF-LOVE JOURNAL FOR TEEN GIRLS

PROMPTS AND PRACTICES TO INSPIRE
CONFIDENCE AND CELEBRATE YOU

CINDY WHITEHEAD

ROCKRIDGE
PRESS

I'd like to dedicate this book to every young person out there who goes after what she/he/they wants and lives an authentic life.

THIS JOURNAL BELONGS TO:

_____

Don't you ever let a soul in the world tell you that you can't be exactly who you are.

—LADY GAGA,

actress, songwriter, and singer

CONTENTS

INTRODUCTION

I'm so glad you picked up this journal! Wherever you are in your life right now, this book is for you. Journaling is fun, and I can tell you firsthand that it works!

I'm Cindy Whitehead, and I was one of the first female pro skateboarders to ride pools and half-pipes back in the day. Skateboarding was (and still is) male-dominated, and I had to have confidence every time I dropped in, knowing that everyone's eyes were on me. I had to believe in myself and know that I belonged right where I was, no matter what other people might say.

I kept a journal throughout those early years for inspiration and to remind myself to stay strong. Those journals helped me work through any problems I faced.

You will have as much fun with this journal as I did with mine. You'll learn about your strengths, how to deal with issues, and how to believe in yourself 100 percent.

What Is Self-Love?

Self-love is about being kind to yourself, no matter what. It means you don't look in the mirror and say negative things about your body or appearance; you don't call yourself names for getting an answer wrong in class. It means you know deep down inside that you deserve the best from people around you—and from yourself.

You know that feeling you get when you know you are going to nail your presentation at school, no matter what happens? That's your confidence kicking in. When someone criticizes you and you're able to let their words just roll right off of you? That's your self-esteem. When you refuse to surround yourself with anyone who takes advantage of you or treats you poorly? That's knowing your self-worth. All of this is part of self-love.

These are skills, and they don't always come easily. But everyone is capable of feeling self-love. It just takes practice—and that's where this journal comes in.

You are incredibly smart, capable, and valuable, and this book is going to remind you of that every time you open it.

How to Use This Book

This rad book has 100 positive affirmations to help you dive deep into exploring your confidence, awareness, and self-love. Affirmations are positive statements that you can use to overcome doubt and fear, instill confidence, and banish negative thoughts. Affirmations are a powerful tool and an important part of your journey.

The affirmations you will see throughout this journal inspire each writing prompt. Read the affirmation aloud, think about it, and then fill in your journal entry. There is no right or wrong here—enjoy the process!

For each affirmation, grab your colored pencils, soft-tip markers, or pastels and color in those words. Just don't use a heavy marker that will bleed through to the next page.

You'll also find lots of creative activities throughout this journal to help put those self-love affirmations and writing prompts into practice.

Let's get started! Have fun with it, explore, let the words and activities sink into you, and let your thoughts and writing flow out of you, because the best thing about this journal is that it is YOURS!

I Am Aware of My Awesome Self

Self-awareness is at the core of self-love, and it can be eye-opening. It is about getting to know what makes you excited and motivated, plus your beliefs, your likes, and your dislikes. It is not about who you *think* you should be. It is about who you are at your core. It is about uncovering the true you. You'll want to put aside what everyone else is doing and tap into what *you* want to do, say, and be. The prompts and affirmations in this section will help you think about yourself honestly and with positivity and curiosity, not criticism or judgment.

I AM AUTHENTIC

You know how there are authentic fashion brands and copy-cat fashion brands? The same is true for people. When you are truly your authentic self, you are not trying to be a copycat version of anyone else or what you think will make you popular. It is genuinely who you are, and because there is no one else 100 percent like you, embracing your authenticity is something to celebrate.

To me, being my authentic self means I

wear what I like despite what others may say or think. I am my sporty self and laugh and smile a ton. I care about others and don't care what other people think. I am a tomboy who wears leggings, joggers, & sweats no jeans, skirts, and/or dresses.

I AM SMART

We all have things we are smart about, and it doesn't necessarily have anything to do with getting good grades. Think about the good decisions you make, the things you know or do well, what you bring to a conversation—all those things are you being "smart." Not everyone is smart in the same way.

I am smart because I can

make good decisions and am pretty okay at school and was in higher level classes & got good grades in those classes along with my other classes.

I ACCEPT MYSELF

At times, we all make mistakes or do not feel we are at our best. Sometimes we try our hardest and still don't achieve our goals. Accepting yourself means you know that you did what you could, and whatever the outcome, you are still *you*, and you are okay with that.

Something that I accept about myself is

_____

_____

_____

_____

_____

_____

_____

_____

_____

_____

_____

_____

I CELEBRATE MY LIFE

Celebrating your life is about focusing on even the small things that make you happy. You don't need to wait for anyone else to celebrate you, nor do you need to wait to achieve a big goal. You can celebrate anything about yourself at any time. It can even be as simple as getting up in the morning, looking in the mirror, and celebrating the fact that you have a new day ahead of you.

I celebrate _____ **about myself.**

In order to celebrate myself I will continue to

_____

_____

_____

_____

_____

_____

_____

_____

_____

_____

-☼- Self-Awareness Letter -☼-

Use the lines below to write a letter to yourself about anything you may have said or done in the past that you regret. You can also include things you may have said no to, due to fear, that you wish you had said yes to. Allow yourself to feel that regret as you write the letter. When you are finished writing, give yourself permission to be free from those mistakes and let them go. Moving forward while acknowledging our past helps us grow and become more self-aware.

_____

_____

_____

_____

_____

_____

_____

_____

_____

_____

_____

_____

_____

_____

_____

I CHANGE MY FEELINGS BY CHANGING MY THOUGHTS

Sometimes it seems like our feelings have complete control over us, but they don't have to. You have the power to change your feelings by changing your thought process. If you start feeling hurt or angry because of something a friend said or did, you have the power to say to yourself, "Until we can talk this out, I am going to chalk it up to her having a bad day." That shifts the negative feeling of "Oh, she hates me!" to a positive thought of "We will try to work this out." And that makes you feel more grounded.

When I feel _____ ,

I change my thoughts to _____ .

This helps me _____

_____

_____

_____

_____

_____

I DO WHAT IS RIGHT FOR ME

Doing what is right for you comes from knowing yourself. It means you do not get led astray when others want to do something that doesn't fit with what you think is right. You have faith that your choices are good ones, and you stick to them.

I did _____

when everyone else _____ .

Doing this made me feel _____

_____

_____

_____

_____

_____

_____

_____

_____

_____

I SHARE MYSELF FEARLESSLY

Sharing yourself fearlessly means not worrying about what people will think of you. It is marching to the beat of your own drummer and expressing your personality. It is giving your true self to those around you and not holding back. You are open to sharing who you really are and do so without fear or regret.

Someone I have shared myself fearlessly with is

_____ .

When I share myself fearlessly, I feel _____

_____

_____

_____

_____

_____

_____

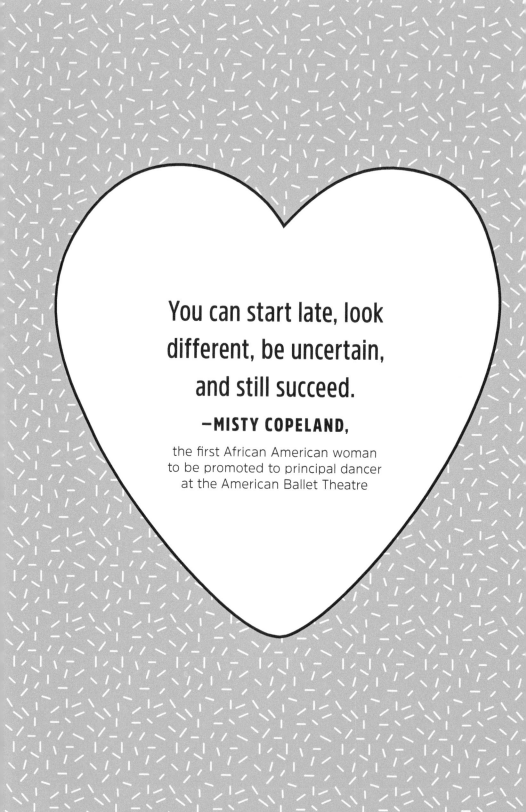

You can start late, look
different, be uncertain,
and still succeed.

—MISTY COPELAND,

the first African American woman
to be promoted to principal dancer
at the American Ballet Theatre

I SHOW PEOPLE WHO I AM

Showing people who you are can come from small actions, like the way you choose to dress and wear your hair, or big ones, like when and how you speak up about things that matter to you. You can show people who you are by being supportive when they're in difficult situations, performing kind acts, keeping confidences, and much more. All the things you say and do show others who you really are.

When I _____ ,

I show people who I am. When I do this, I feel

_____

_____

_____

_____

_____

_____

_____

_____

I RADIATE CONFIDENCE

When you feel confident, you can walk into a room and know you belong. You can raise your hand and ask a question in class, believing you have every right to express your curiosity and seek an answer. If you are not quite there yet, act with confidence, and the feelings will follow. Hold your head high and tell yourself, "You got this!" Radiating confidence shows those around you that you are self-assured and know who you are.

The last time I radiated confidence was when I _____ .

I find it easy to be confident when _____ .

I struggle to feel confident when _____ .

One thing I can do to make myself feel more confident is

_____

_____

_____

_____

_____

_____

_____

I AM PEACEFUL

Sometimes life puts us in stressful situations. We can't stop that from happening, but we *can* train ourselves to respond to these situations more calmly. When you learn to be at peace with whatever life may throw at you, you make better decisions and do not act under stress. Some people find meditation and journaling to be helpful in keeping the peace.

The way I create a peaceful life for myself is by

_____

_____

_____

_____

_____

_____

_____

_____

_____

_____

_____

I ENJOY MY JOURNEY

Your life is a journey, and you can enjoy it the whole way through. If you get too focused on outcomes—getting into a college, landing a job, winning a contest, getting a prom date—you might forget to appreciate all the steps along the way. Just like in your favorite book or movie, there are so many things to enjoy throughout your personal journey, even when it takes longer than you'd wanted or goes in directions you hadn't expected.

A personal journey I recently went on was

_____

_____

_____

_____

_____

My favorite parts of this journey were

_____

_____

_____

_____

_____

Confidence on Display

In each of the five heart shapes below, write in a word that shows what you are confident about, using a colored pencil or felt-tip pen to make strong, broad strokes.

BEING MY TRUE SELF MAKES ME HAPPY

Allowing yourself to be the true YOU is good for your self-esteem and your emotions. When we hide who we really are, it can cause negative feelings and unhappiness that filter into our daily actions. Being the authentic version of yourself allows you to be more present and happier with yourself and others.

I know I am my true self when I

_____

_____

_____

_____

_____

_____

_____

_____

_____

_____

I AM ENOUGH

Say this one out loud and over and over . . . and over again. Knowing deep inside that you are enough gives you inner strength and protects you from harsh judgment. Being you is just right. You are not lacking in any qualities—you are enough just the way you are!

Because I am enough, I can

_____

_____

_____

_____

_____

_____

_____

_____

_____

_____

_____

I AM THE ARCHITECT OF MY LIFE

You are the one building this life of yours. *You*—not your parents or friends—decide where you are heading, how you will get there, and how you feel. Each and every day, you are adding pieces that shape your life. It is like writing your own story—you have the power to create this masterpiece any way you want to.

I am building a life that

_____

_____

_____

_____

_____

_____

_____

_____

_____

_____

-̇- **Time to Chill** -̇-

Make a list and draw three simple activities you can do at home that help you stay peaceful.

1.
_____

_____

2.
_____

_____

3.
_____

_____

I AM BOLD

Being bold is powerful. At times, being bold can be scary, but that doesn't mean it's wrong. You are giving yourself permission to face the world with strength and paint your vision in broad, beautiful strokes. You are being bold with your choices, your voice, and your actions.

The boldest thing I have ever done is

_____

_____

_____

_____

_____

_____

_____

_____

_____

_____

_____

_____

I DREAM BIG

Dreams help us get to know what's really important to us. When we dream, we reach for the stars and imagine all the possibilities for what we can do in life. The bigger those dreams are, the better—nothing is off-limits here. Dreams turn into goals, and we get to go after them. No one can take your dreams away from you.

A dream I have is to

_____

_____

_____

_____

Some steps I could take to pursue this dream are

_____

_____

_____

_____

_____

_____

MY DIFFERENCES ARE MY STRENGTHS

You are unique. That is an amazing thing. By embracing your individuality, you become confident and understand that the things that make you different are also the things that make you valuable and irreplaceable. You celebrate your differences, because they're what makes you who you are.

A time I embraced my unique individuality was

_____

_____

_____

_____

_____

_____

_____

_____

_____

_____

_____

_____

I AM AWARE

Awareness comes from really watching and listening to the world and people around you. When you closely pay attention to what people say, do, and need, it can help you be a better friend or ally. If a friend says they are "fine," but you can tell by their body language they are clearly not, *that* is awareness. Being aware allows you to have better relationships with those around you.

Because I am aware, I have noticed that

_____

_____

_____

_____

_____

_____

_____

_____

_____

_____

⇥ **Dream Big** ⇤

Fill these clouds with your biggest dreams—you can use words to describe them, or you can draw them!

I AM FREE

When you are free, you do not feel weighed down. You can start feeling free from anxiety by accepting what you cannot change. You can free yourself from negativity by empowering yourself to think positive thoughts. You can free yourself from grudges by encouraging yourself to let go of any resentments. Even when other people place rules on you, you have an internal freedom over your own mind that nobody can take away.

I am free because I let go of

_____

_____

_____

_____

_____

_____

_____

_____

_____

_____

_____

I AM GROWING

We grow by listening to others and trying to understand where they are coming from. We also grow by trying new things and learning what is best for us. Growth helps us move ahead in our life and know more about ourselves. The more you grow, the wiser you are, and the less you have to be afraid of.

One way I've grown recently is that I

_____

_____

_____

_____

_____

_____

_____

_____

_____

_____

_____

_____

I USE MY WORDS WISELY

Words are powerful. Your words can uplift someone or bring them down. This includes when you talk to yourself! If you are thoughtful and considerate with your words, you can make other people (and yourself) feel comfortable and supported.

I used my words wisely when I

_____

_____

_____

_____

_____

_____

_____

_____

_____

_____

_____

No one was going to stop me from writing . . . It was natural, really, that I would take that interest.

—OCTAVIA BUTLER,

Hugo and Nebula Award–winning science fiction author

I LOVE MYSELF

You are 100 percent worthy of love. If you love yourself, then the love of others may follow. And by loving yourself, you're learning how to love other people. You can be kind, understanding, and accepting of others once you have learned how to love yourself. Do you know the saying "it starts with you"? It really does.

Some of the things I love most about myself are

_____

_____

_____

_____

_____

_____

_____

_____

_____

_____

_____

I STAND UP FOR MYSELF

When we stand up for ourselves, we are helping other people understand our wants and needs and respect our boundaries. The things you want and need are legitimate, and you don't have to make any excuses for them. You don't let anyone steamroll past your boundaries without your consent.

I stand up for myself by

_____

_____

_____

_____

_____

When I stand up for myself, I feel

_____

_____

_____

_____

_____

_____

I LIVE IN THE PRESENT

You cannot change the past, and you cannot control the future. Instead, you focus on being the best person you can be today. You participate fully in whatever is going on right this minute, and you appreciate the experiences you're having as they unfold.

Living in the present makes _____

better. When I live in the present, I _____

_____ .

When I find myself getting caught up in regrets about the past or worries about the future, I

_____

_____

_____

_____

_____

_____

_____

I LEARN FROM MY MISTAKES

We all make mistakes. If we didn't, we would not grow or become self-aware. Admitting that you made a mistake is brave, and learning from your mistakes is how you avoid repeating them. It also helps you figure out how to tackle the situation differently next time.

_____

_____ was a mistake I learned a lot

from. Moving forward, I plan on _____

_____

_____

_____

_____

_____

_____

_____

_____

⚡ Bad Feelings, Be Gone! ⚡

Sit on your bed, cross your legs, close your eyes, and picture a scenario where you felt upset, sad, mad, or uneasy. Now fill in the blanks below to help guide you in what you can do moving forward to shake off those negative emotions.

When _____ happened,

at first it made me feel _____,

and I reacted by _____.

When I acted _____, it made me feel

_____, which was _____.

Next time _____ happens to me, I will think of

_____ and then do _____.

I will not _____ or _____,

and if things don't go my way, I will then _____.

I will also remember that _____

and to _____.

_____

_____

_____

_____

PART

2

I Am So Worth It

Your self-worth comes from knowing that you are good enough, important, necessary, and worthy of people's time and love—including your own. You know that you belong exactly where you are. You don't base your opinion of yourself on what others say about you. You are confident in your feelings, thoughts, and opinions. Self-worth gives you the confidence to say no to things that aren't right for you and to speak up when you need to. The affirmations and prompts in this section will help give you an even deeper understanding of your own self-worth.

I AM CREATIVE

Some of the best ideas come from thinking creatively: doing things differently from others, following the path others choose to ignore, being curious, and trying new things, even if they are out of your comfort zone. As a creative person, you don't see challenges as roadblocks—you see them as opportunities to try something new.

The last time I felt creative I did

_____

_____

_____

_____

I use my creativity to

_____

_____

_____

_____

_____

I AM COURAGEOUS

Being courageous is not about having a lack of fear. You can be courageous and still be afraid, but the trick is overcoming what you are worried or scared about and then taking action. Maybe trying out for a sports team or play seems scary, but you take a deep breath and do it anyway. That is you being courageous.

When I am courageous, it makes me feel

_____

_____

_____

_____

_____

One of the courageous things I've done is

_____

_____

_____

_____

_____

_____

_____

I AM DETERMINED

Determination comes from your inner strength. You have a thought, a plan, or an action you wish to take, and you figure out how to make it happen. When you're confronted with obstacles, you work hard to overcome them. The positive feeling of determination helps motivate you to reach that goal.

Something I feel determined about doing is

_____

_____

_____

_____

_____

_____

_____

_____

_____

_____

_____

_____

I AM FEARLESS

When you are fearless, you are unafraid to speak your mind, be yourself, or show who you truly are to others. This comes from knowing your self-worth. The first step to being fearless is remembering that you are enough and that your thoughts and words are important.

Being fearless means that I am able to

_____

_____

_____

_____

_____

_____

_____

_____

_____

_____

_____

_____

_____

☀ Face Your Fears! ☀

Inside the circle of the sun, write down a dream you have in big, bold words. Now, on the rays of the sun, write in tiny letters the fears that are in your way. Look at how small those fear words are and how powerful your dream is. When you put your fear into perspective, it does not seem so scary.

I AM GENEROUS

It is important to be generous with those around you *and* with yourself. When you are generous, you give freely. You make allowances for mistakes, and you give yourself and others the benefit of the doubt. You can be generous to others by sharing your time, listening, or physically helping. You can be generous to yourself by giving yourself a break when you need one and rewarding yourself when you feel that you have done an excellent job.

To me, being generous means that I

_____

_____

When I'm generous to myself, I

_____

_____

When I'm generous to others, I

_____

_____

_____

_____

I AM ALWAYS LEARNING

Every day we learn new things from all sorts of sources: books, experiences, and other people. The goal isn't to know everything—it's to be eager to discover what you do not yet know. When you open yourself up to watching and listening to what is happening around you, you learn to broaden your range of compassion, emotions, and knowledge.

Some things I have learned lately are

_____

_____

_____

_____

_____

When I learn something new, I

_____

_____

_____

_____

_____

I AM LOVED

Knowing that you are loved is a big part of your self-worth. Different people demonstrate that they love you in so many different ways: by how they treat you, the time they spend, the way they listen to what you have to say, and the respect they give you. Take the time to notice how your friends and family members show you their love.

I know I am loved because

_____

_____

_____

_____

_____

People in my life show me that they love me by

_____

_____

_____

_____

_____

_____

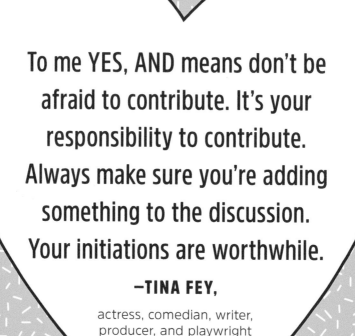

To me YES, AND means don't be afraid to contribute. It's your responsibility to contribute. Always make sure you're adding something to the discussion. Your initiations are worthwhile.

—TINA FEY,

actress, comedian, writer, producer, and playwright

I AM PERSISTENT

Sometimes people mistake persistence for being pushy or stubborn. It really is not either of those things. It is not a negative. Persistence is pushing forward even if you are discouraged. You hold your ground and inch toward your goal.

When I am persistent, the outcome is usually

_____

_____

_____

_____

_____

_____

I am persistent because _____

_____

_____

_____

_____

_____

_____

I AM POWERFUL

Unlike what we often see on TV and in the movies, power does not come from ruling over people or having the upper hand. It comes from your ability to have a positive effect on yourself and those around you. You carry the power within you to make any situation more fair and right.

Being powerful means that I can

_____

_____

_____

_____

_____

_____

_____

_____

_____

_____

_____

_____

I AM READY

Being ready is your mental strength of knowing that whatever happens, you will be okay. You trust yourself to have thought out possible scenarios and plans of action for situations that may arise and to be able to think on your feet and respond to whatever surprises might come up. When you know that you're ready, you don't have to feel anxious.

I am ready to

_____

_____

_____

_____

_____

I get myself ready for tough situations by

_____

_____

_____

_____

_____

_____

I AM WHOLE

Being whole means that you embrace the qualities you have and that you know your potential is endless. When you are whole, you focus on the positive and are happy with who you are. You are complete in every sense of the word, in mind, body, and spirit. You don't need any external validation—you know you have everything you need in and of yourself.

I am whole because I

_____

_____

_____

_____

_____

_____

_____

_____

_____

_____

☀ **Celebrate Your Uniqueness!** ☀

It could be your singing voice. Maybe you can remember every-one's birthday. Perhaps it's how you wear your hair. Maybe you surf or skateboard or you read the dictionary for fun. What-ever the things are that make you unique, let's celebrate them! In each of the five stars below, write one thing that makes you special.

I AM UNIQUE

You are one of a kind, and how great is that? There is no one else exactly like you out there in the world—and there never will be! Your voice, your body, your mind, and your thoughts are all unique to you and you alone. Nobody else can ever take your place.

Some things that make me unique are

_____

_____

_____

_____

_____

_____

_____

_____

_____

_____

_____

_____

I AM WORTHY OF LOVE

Everyone is worthy of love. *Everyone*. You deserve to be loved. Why? Because you are human and you are doing your best. It doesn't matter that you've made mistakes. You don't have to be perfect to be loved—you just have to be yourself.

I know I am worthy of love because

_____

_____

_____

_____

_____

_____

_____

_____

_____

_____

_____

I ACCEPT COMPLIMENTS EASILY

Accepting compliments easily means you not only believe in yourself and the praise others are giving you, but you also are giving others assurance that they are right. You are making them feel good about giving you a compliment. If someone said, "I love your big, beautiful smile!" and you responded with, "Ugh. I hate my teeth, and my mouth is too wide," you would be negating what was said to you. That wouldn't make you *or* the compliment-giver feel good. When you respond instead with "Thank you," you *both* get a burst of positive feelings.

The last time I received a compliment I

_____

_____

_____

The best compliment I've received was

_____

_____

_____

_____

⚡ I Love Compliments ⚡

In the 10 blanks provided below, write 10 different compliments you have received. Come back to this list as often as needed to remember how amazing you are and give yourself a little confidence boost in the process.

1. _____

2. _____

3. _____

4. _____

5. _____

6. _____

7. _____

8. _____

9. _____

10. _____

I BELONG IN ANY SPACE I WALK INTO

Belonging, no matter where you are, is about believing in yourself and having confidence. You should never feel that any place or group of people is better than you, for any reason at all. You belong wherever you choose to go.

When I walk into a space and know I belong, I feel

_____

_____

_____

_____

When I feel like I don't belong somewhere, I make myself feel better by

_____

_____

_____

_____

_____

_____

_____

I CAN ACHIEVE ANYTHING

You are capable of amazing things! Nothing is out of reach for you. The only limits are the ones you put on yourself. No one else can put those limits on you unless you allow them to. With clear goals and a strong will, you can achieve anything you set your mind and heart to!

When I _____ **, I was able**

to achieve _____

_____

_____

_____

_____

_____

_____

_____

_____

_____

_____

_____

I DESERVE HAPPINESS

Happiness is not something that you earn or that only certain people are entitled to. It's an emotion we all deserve just by being alive. When you're happy, you radiate positivity and have more energy. Life feels better, and you treat yourself and others around you with more kindness, compassion, understanding, and love.

I know I deserve to be happy because

_____

_____

_____

_____

When I am happy, I

_____

_____

_____

_____

_____

I HAVE THE POWER TO CREATE CHANGE

Did you know that if you disagree with something, your actions and words have the power to create change? You don't have to stand idly by if you witness an injustice. When you see something wrong, you have the power to speak up and to encourage others to do the same. Ordinary people saying that they will not accept things is how all change begins.

I saw that I have the power to create change when I

_____

_____

_____

_____

A policy, habit, or custom that I changed was _____

_____ .

I made this change by

_____

_____

_____

_____

⫶ Be Powerful, Create Change! ⫶

At marches, people carry signs and posters signifying ways they want to create change in this world. In the sign below, write or draw in the change *you* would like to make happen. Remember that you have the power!

I MAKE A DIFFERENCE IN MY COMMUNITY

You can make a difference by listening, giving, or doing. All of these actions show that you care and can have a positive effect on those you choose to help. Maybe you help a classmate struggling with homework, make signs for a peaceful protest, clean up a local park, or volunteer for an organization you believe in. There are many ways, big and small, to make a difference.

My next plan for making a difference is

_____

_____

_____

_____

I have previously made a positive difference in my community by

_____

_____

_____

_____

I MAKE A DIFFERENCE IN THE WORLD

Just by being here, you are making a difference in this world. You don't always know whether the impact of your actions will be small or large, so always try to act with kindness and generosity. You never know how far your influence will spread. Whatever positive actions you choose each day, you are making a difference in the world.

I did _____

_____ ,

and that made a difference in the world because _____

_____

_____

_____

_____

_____

_____

_____

_____

I MATTER

Your opinions are valuable. You are smart, kind, and loving. You respect yourself and others. You choose to do things to make life better for yourself and those around you. Remind yourself that every single thing you do matters. Your whole self matters!

I remind myself that I matter by

_____

_____

_____

_____

_____

_____

_____

_____

_____

_____

_____

_____

I feel like dreams are always a little tricky, you know. But if you just push through the struggles and the hard times, it'll be so worth it in the end, because you will be able to get to your dreams.

—CHLOE KIM,

the youngest woman to win an Olympic snowboarding gold medal

I OVERCOME MY FEARS

Many people feel afraid to follow their dreams, because they are scared of failure, getting hurt, making mistakes, being teased, or not achieving what they desire. Overcome those fears by setting mini goals and asking yourself, *What am I afraid of? How do I push through that fear?* When you work through your concerns, a dream can become a reality. And that is a great feeling!

By _____

_____ ,

I overcame my fear of _____

_____

to follow my dream of _____

_____

_____

_____

_____

_____

_____

I RESPECT MYSELF

When you respect yourself and your self-worth, you know what is and is not right for you. You respect yourself enough not to do things that cause you harm. You are honest with yourself about who you are and what you value, and you don't allow others to push your boundaries.

I respect myself by

_____

_____

_____

_____

_____

_____

_____

_____

_____

_____

_____

_____

I WILL FIGURE IT OUT

Sometimes we don't know things, and that is okay. You trust that you have the skills you need to do what it takes to understand the situation, solve the problem, or find the answer. You are confident that you will use your best judgment to figure out what is best for you in every situation. You don't leave important things to chance or to others to decide for you.

I have had to figure out problems by

_____

_____

_____

_____

_____

_____

_____

_____

_____

_____

_____

_____

I DESERVE GOOD THINGS

When good things happen to you, it is often due to what you put out into the world. Positivity, hard work, and determination all play a part in bringing good things into your life. Other times, it feels like good things happen to you just because of random luck—you deserve those, too. You are entitled to all of them just by being yourself. Embrace the good things and be happy about them as they happen.

I know that I deserve good things because

_____

_____

_____

_____

_____

When good things happen to me, I feel

_____

_____

_____

_____

_____

⫯ Things That Make Me Happy ⫯

Use colored pencils to draw some of the things that make you happy. Get as creative as you can—there is no right or wrong for what brings you joy.

I Respect My Awesome Self

When you respect yourself, you understand that your needs are valuable. Because you respect yourself, you won't accept anything less than respectful treatment from others. You know that you are good and worthy of always being treated well. Your personal boundaries are strong and firm, and you do not hesitate to correct those around you if they cross those boundaries. The affirmations and prompts in this section will help you stand up for yourself and make sure others treat you with the respect you deserve.

I AM BRAVE

Being brave is something you probably do in small ways every single day. Do you smile at people you don't know yet? That's being brave. Do you stick up for others when people bully them? That is a bigger act of bravery. Practice small acts of bravery daily, and you will soon notice the bigger things you do that make you brave.

I felt brave when I

_____

_____

_____

_____

_____

_____

_____

_____

_____

_____

_____

_____

I AM CONFIDENT

You can demonstrate confidence by walking into situations with your head held high, looking people in the eye when you are speaking, or waiting your turn and then speaking up and voicing your opinion. Even when you are *not* feeling your most confident, you can use small techniques like these to pretend that you are. And once you pretend hard enough, you'll start to feel it, too.

The last time I showed my confidence was when I

_____

_____

_____

_____

_____

_____

_____

_____

_____

_____

I AM COMPASSIONATE

Having compassion means that you are in tune with others' emotions, and you offer them the benefit of the doubt. You have sensitivity for what they may be going through. You can also have compassion for yourself, for example by not being too hard on yourself when you tried and tried with all your might but still fell short of a goal. Self-compassion is the opposite of beating yourself up. You give yourself and others a safe place to feel whatever emotion they (or you) are going through.

Compassion, for me, is

_____

_____

_____

_____

_____

_____

_____

_____

_____

_____

_____

I AM CURIOUS

Curiosity fuels learning. By being curious, we can find out all sorts of things. If you're curious to know why people and situations are the way they are, then you're not approaching them with judgment but instead with a genuine desire to understand. We can even use our curiosity to find out more about ourselves. By being curious, you gain knowledge and start having a better understanding of where you stand on issues, your opinions, your body, and more.

I was curious about _____

_____ .

To better understand it, I

_____

_____

_____

_____

_____

_____

_____

_____

-ᛡ- **The Circles of Trust** -ᛡ-

In the circles below, write three words that you feel make a person trustworthy. Use different colored pens or colored pencils for each of the three words. When you write them down, read the words aloud and see how each relates to building trust. We call this *the circles of trust,* because whatever is inside is part of a bond that cannot be broken.

I AM EMPOWERED

When you trust and believe in yourself, you know that you have the power within you to do whatever needs to be done. You have the ability, confidence, and clarity to make good decisions. You can carry out your ideas, protect your boundaries, and set the tone for how you want those around you to treat you. Being empowered makes you feel confident in your choices.

The last time I felt empowered was

_____

_____

_____

_____

_____

_____

_____

_____

_____

_____

_____

_____

I AM GRATEFUL

You see the things you have accomplished, what you have, the people who care for you, and your abilities, and you are appreciative of them. You are thankful for what you have and not focused on what you do not have. Being grateful keeps you in the present and happy with what you have right now.

I am grateful for

_____

_____

_____

_____

_____

_____

_____

_____

_____

_____

_____

I AM IMAGINATIVE

Let your imagination run wild! Why? Because that means you can form new thoughts and ideas, which are great not only for problem-solving but also for creating a future that you want to be part of. Being imaginative can take you places in your mind that are wonderful, beautiful, fun, and colorful. Imagining something is the first step to making it real.

My imagination helps me

_____

_____

_____

_____

_____

_____

_____

_____

_____

_____

_____

_____

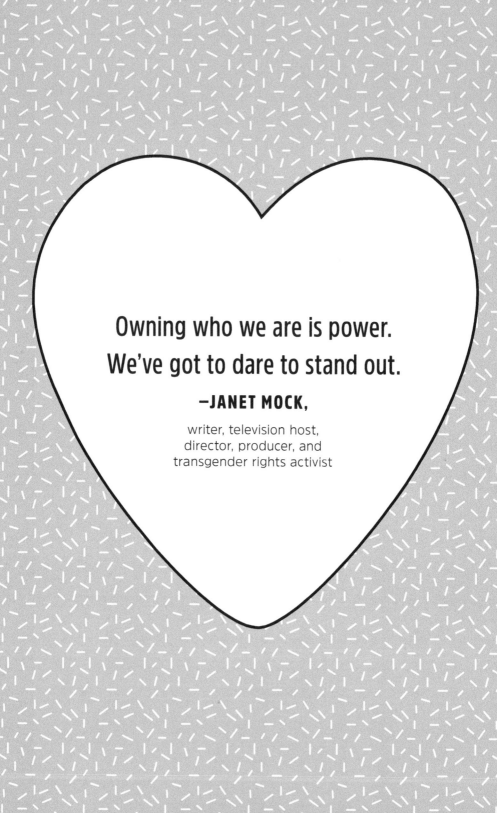

Owning who we are is power.
We've got to dare to stand out.

—JANET MOCK,

writer, television host,
director, producer, and
transgender rights activist

I AM KIND

Kindness is very important in this world—not only extending kindness to others but also being kind to yourself. When you are truly kind, you do not expect anything in return. You can extend a kind word, a helping hand, or a shoulder to lean on. Being kind makes others feel good and, in turn, boosts your energy as well.

My favorite ways to be kind are

_____

_____

_____

_____

_____

_____

_____

_____

_____

_____

_____

_____

I AM MYSELF

Being yourself is knowing the true you and sticking to it. When you hide who you are because you want to fit in or are scared of what people might think, it is like you are playing a part. Embracing your true self is far more freeing and fulfilling.

When I am myself, I

_____

_____

_____

_____

_____

_____

_____

_____

_____

_____

_____

_____

I AM PERFECTLY IMPERFECT

You've probably heard before that "nobody's perfect," and it's true. We all have our flaws, and that's not a problem. Sometimes what you see as a flaw in yourself may actually be a strength. Being perfectly imperfect means you will make mistakes. You will have days when you may not feel put together on the outside or the inside, and that is okay!

Something "imperfect" that I love about myself is

_____

_____

_____

_____

_____

_____

_____

_____

_____

_____

_____

_____

I AM THANKFUL

If you can wake up each day and find just three things you are thankful for, you are starting the day off right. If your day doesn't go as planned, you can remember those three things and remember that things are not as rough as they may seem. Being thankful gives you perspective and helps you focus not on the low points but on the positives.

I am thankful for

_____

_____

_____

_____

_____

_____

_____

_____

_____

_____

_____

⊰ How Many Things Are You Grateful For? ⊱

Every night before you go to sleep, reflect on the things you are grateful for. Place a small empty jar beside your bed. Place a penny or small rock inside the jar for every grateful moment you had that day. Write down some of those things on the page below, and see how many things you are grateful for by the end of the week.

I AM TRUSTWORTHY

You are dependable, reliable, and honest. People know that your word is gold. If you say you will do something, you will. You never need to be told twice; you just follow through. When you promise to keep a secret, your friends know that you mean it. Being trustworthy is important, because once you break people's trust, it is tough to get it back.

I know I am trustworthy because I

_____

_____

_____

_____

_____

_____

_____

_____

_____

_____

_____

I BELIEVE IN MYSELF

Believing in yourself is powerful. When you do this, you can make so much happen. You trust in your ideas, your capabilities, your thoughts, and your actions. You know that you can do whatever you put your mind to. When you believe in yourself, you can overcome fear, self-doubt, and any other obstacle in your way.

Believing in myself helped me accomplish

_____

_____

_____

_____

_____

_____

_____

_____

_____

_____

I CAN DO
HARD THINGS

Doing hard things helps you grow as a person. It bolsters your self-esteem. When you accomplish something that is hard for you, it feels amazing—even better than when you accomplish something that came easily. Just because something is challenging, that doesn't mean you should give up. Keep going. You got this!

The last hard thing I did was

_____

_____

_____

_____

_____

_____

_____

_____

_____

_____

_____

÷ **Being Kind Is Cool** ÷

Below is a blank postcard. Write a note to a friend and say some kind things about them. It can be as simple as you liked their outfit or the way they play sports. Or you can go deeper and add compliments about how smart they are or how easily they make friends. Make it honest and heartfelt. Moving forward, practice saying some of these things to them in person. When you are kind, people feel better and so do you!

I DO MY BEST

When you do your best, you leave nothing on the table. Even if you don't achieve your goal or win that prize, you can be extremely proud and have no regrets. Don't compare your own best on any given day to anyone else's. Some days you have more resources than others, and you do as much as you can with whatever you have.

When I do my best, I feel

_____

_____

_____

_____

_____

_____

_____

_____

_____

_____

_____

I FORGIVE MYSELF

Sometimes you will realize that you said or did something wrong and you feel bad about it. Forgiving yourself is an important thing to know how to do. You can start by reminding yourself that everyone makes mistakes and that no one is perfect. Understand why you acted the way you did, figure out how you will do better going forward, and forgive yourself. That's how a mistake or a bad choice turns into a learning opportunity.

I forgive myself for

_____

_____

_____

_____

_____

_____

_____

_____

_____

_____

_____

I LET GO OF NEGATIVE SELF-TALK

Have you ever looked in the mirror and said something mean to yourself about your body or looks? What about calling yourself names because you forgot to do something or didn't know the answer on a test? That is negative self-talk. Next time you start to do this, ask yourself, "Would I speak to my best friend this way?" You can bet the answer to that is a strong no. Next time you catch yourself doing this, replace that negative self-talk with affirmations from this book. Treat yourself with kindness and positive words, just as you would the people you love.

Instead of negative self-talk, I tell myself that I am

_____

_____

_____

_____

_____

_____

_____

I LOVE MY BODY

Your body is beautiful! It takes you places you want to go. It has a wonderful mind and a unique shape, and every inch of it is yours. No two people have the exact same body, so celebrate and love yours in its entirety. Try not to compare yourself to others—instead, remind yourself that every type of body is the right type of body.

The thing I love most about my body is

_____

_____

_____

_____

_____

_____

_____

_____

_____

_____

_____

⊰ No Negatives, Just Positives! ⊱

Use the blank space below to draw a picture of yourself. You can look in the mirror as you draw yourself if that helps. You can draw just the outline of your body or go into more detail if you like. After you have the shape of your body drawn, start writing positive words and arrows pointing to each part of your body.

I OVERCOME DIFFICULTIES

There are things we can control and things we cannot. Overcoming difficulties that we can control requires problem-solving and action. Overcoming challenges outside of our control may involve meditation, adjusting our perspective, or accepting the circumstances. Asking for help is another way we can try to overcome difficulties. When you overcome an obstacle, you feel stronger and more capable.

The last difficulty I faced was _____

_____ ,

and to overcome it, I _____

_____

_____

_____

_____

_____

_____

_____

I SPEAK UP

Speaking up can be hard, sometimes even scary. But it's worth it, because you have something valuable to say. Holding it in doesn't allow others to get to know the real you or to benefit from your perspective. Speaking up can involve raising your hand in class, voicing your opinion with friends, or standing up and speaking out in public. When you speak up, you have the power to have an impact on the people around you.

When I speak up, I feel that people

_____

_____

_____

_____

_____

_____

_____

_____

_____

_____

I STAND UP FOR OTHERS

Standing up for others is a generous and empowering thing to do. It's what you would want someone else to do for you. Maybe someone is getting picked on, and you say something on their behalf. Or perhaps you voice your opinion about groups of people who are not being treated fairly in the world. There are many ways to stand up for others, and they'll make you *and* the people you're supporting feel good.

Standing up for others is important to me because

_____

_____

_____

_____

_____

I have stood up for others by

_____

_____

_____

_____

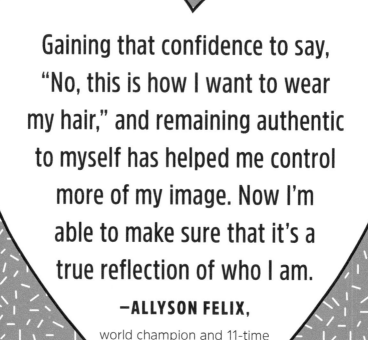

Gaining that confidence to say, "No, this is how I want to wear my hair," and remaining authentic to myself has helped me control more of my image. Now I'm able to make sure that it's a true reflection of who I am.

—ALLYSON FELIX,

world champion and 11-time
Olympic medalist in
track and field

I TRUST MYSELF

Trusting yourself involves confidence, being aware of your feelings and thoughts, and sticking to what you believe is the right decision for you. When you trust yourself, you can make good decisions and throw out self-doubt that sometimes wants to creep in. Trusting yourself can mean you know when to leave the party, or the amount of time to set aside to get your homework done, or when to listen instead of speaking.

I trust myself to

_____

_____

_____

_____

_____

_____

_____

_____

_____

_____

I BELIEVE IN THE POWER OF YET

Almost nothing is final. Things change all the time. Understanding that is what allows us to move forward and have hope. Believing in *yet* gives us the energy and inclination to trust that good things are coming! When we believe in the power of *yet*, we give ourselves the knowledge that things may not have happened yet, but they can and hopefully will as we move forward.

Believing in the power of *yet* means I

_____

_____

_____

_____

_____

_____

_____

_____

_____

_____

I AM AWESOME

Believing that you are awesome doesn't mean that you are conceited. It means that you know that you are capable, hard-working, smart, kind, and imaginative and that you make things happen. Knowing that you are awesome is an *awesome* confidence booster!

I know I am awesome because

_____

_____

_____

_____

_____

_____

_____

_____

_____

_____

_____

_____

I DON'T WORRY ABOUT THINGS I CANNOT CONTROL

Sometimes in this world, there are things that are simply out of our control. We can worry ourselves sick about them, or we can have the power to understand that this time, we have to be calm and go with the flow a bit. For instance, you may not have control over which classroom and teacher you are assigned to. You can recognize that this is something you have no control over and adapt to the situation and make the best of it. When we do this, we feel calmer and more peaceful, and we can then focus on what we *can* control, like making some new friends!

I knew _____

_____

was out of my control, so I did

_____

_____

_____

_____

_____

⌁ Write a Love Letter (to Yourself)! ⌁

Write a detailed love letter to yourself—no negative thoughts here! This is not a list—write this letter to yourself as if you were writing to a friend to remind them how great they really are. Think about how you would want them to feel. Make sure you include all the wonderful things you love about yourself: your words, actions, body, and mind. Sometimes we need to look at ourselves from the outside to see just how awesome we truly are.

_____

_____

_____

_____

_____

_____

_____

_____

_____

_____

_____

PART
4

Self-Care Is My Superpower

S elf-care is all about taking care of yourself and prioritizing what you need to be happy and productive. When you practice self-care, you give yourself time to rest, be thoughtful about your own needs, reflect, replenish, and renew your body and mind. You will have more energy and awareness to tackle anything life throws your way. Only when you take care of yourself, both inside and out, are you able to help others. Self-care is where everything we've been talking about—self-awareness, self-worth, and self-respect—comes together. The affirmations and prompts in this section will help you tap into your needs and find ways to nourish and nurture your awesome self.

I AM BALANCED

When you are balanced, you feel calm and in control. Your mind is clear, your body is rested, and you don't feel pushed or pulled in too many directions. So how do we get that balanced feeling? By being present. Focusing on past problems or what happens next takes us away from what is happening now. By being present both mentally and physically, we achieve a more balanced perspective.

When I am balanced, I feel

_____

_____

_____

_____

_____

_____

_____

_____

_____

_____

_____

I AM CALM

When you are calm, you can think rationally and make clear-headed decisions. Your actions do not reflect fleeting emotions, and they're not born from fear. In order to get to a calm place, you need to quiet your mind, banish distractions, and go inward to center yourself so you can tune in to your own thoughts. When you feel calm, you also feel at peace.

The things I do to feel calm are

_____

_____

_____

_____

_____

_____

_____

_____

_____

_____

_____

_____

I AM JOYFUL

When you're joyful, you are thankful for the wonderful things in your life. You're motivated to smile, have a positive outlook, and be kind to others and yourself. When you express joy, it can be contagious and give those around you positive vibes as well!

When I am joyful, I express it by

_____

_____

_____

To me, joy feels like

_____

_____

_____

_____

I feel joyful when

_____

_____

_____

_____

I AM LOVING

You care about others, and you show it, whether it's by expressing affection or by listening and being compassionate about what others are going through. You show love to yourself first, and you're able to offer that same kindness, acceptance, and positivity to those around you.

I know I am loving because I

_____

_____

_____

_____

I show my love by

_____

_____

_____

_____

_____

_____

⊰ **Resilience Wins!** ⊱

On the lines provided below, write down a problem you have had recently. Then write down what you did to solve it. Seeing your resilience written down and remembering how you got there will inspire you to do the same next time.

PROBLEM

_____

_____

_____

_____

SOLUTION

_____

_____

_____

_____

_____

_____

_____

_____

I AM MINDFUL

When we are mindful, we are aware of our emotions and thoughts and how we feel physically. We can also take into consideration how others around us are feeling. We know that there is no right or wrong way to feel. We are fully present and in tune with our thoughts in each given moment.

Being mindful makes me feel

_____

_____

_____

_____

_____

Some things I do to practice mindfulness are

_____

_____

_____

_____

_____

I AM POSITIVE

Positivity allows us to see the good in ourselves, others, and our situations. When we have a positive outlook, we feel better and react to the world with curiosity rather than fear. For instance, if you think the new girl at school is mean and dislikes you because she did not say hi, how about thinking, "The new girl must be shy because she does not know anyone here"? That is turning negative thinking into positive thinking.

Having a positive outlook helps me be

_____

_____

_____

_____

_____

_____

_____

_____

_____

_____

_____

I AM PURPOSEFUL

When you live your life with purpose, it gives you a sense of calm and well-being. You know what you're here for. You are acting with compassion and making a positive difference in the world. Being purposeful is about setting realistic goals and working toward them.

Being purposeful makes me realize that

_____

_____

_____

_____

_____

I am purposeful about

_____

_____

_____

_____

_____

Women have to take the time to focus on our mental health—take time for self, for the spiritual, without feeling guilty or selfish. The world will see you the way you see you, and treat you the way you treat yourself.

—BEYONCÉ,

singer, songwriter,
record producer, and actress

I AM RESILIENT

"Bouncing back" and "letting things slide" are phrases we hear throughout our lives. Being resilient is just that. You adapt well when tough stuff happens in your life, whether it's with family, school, friends, health, or anything that may cause you stress. When you are resilient, you roll with the punches, work through the problems, and do not allow adversity to get you down.

When I am resilient, I can

_____

_____

_____

_____

_____

_____

_____

_____

_____

_____

_____

I AM SAFE

Take a deep breath, relax your body, and remind yourself that you are safe. To feel safe, we need to create an environment where our boundaries are strong, we are able to speak up when needed, and we know that we are respected and loved unconditionally. Your safety is the number one most important thing—if you're ever in a situation where you are unsafe, do what you can to remove yourself from that situation immediately.

Feeling safe is important to me because

_____

_____

_____

_____

_____

Some things, people, or places that make me feel safe are

_____

_____

_____

_____

_____

I AM STRONG

Being strong does not mean that you don't show emotions. It means that you keep trying to achieve your goals even if it's hard and you hit roadblocks along the way. You do not quit, because you can look back at where you started and see how far you have already come. You can also be strong for others: you can be a shoulder to lean on or an ear to listen when they are going through the tough stuff. You are stronger than the tough stuff. Being strong helps you get to where you would like to go.

The strong qualities I have are

_____

_____

_____

_____

_____

_____

_____

_____

_____

I CAN SAY NO

When you were a little child, you probably said no a lot. It may have been one of your first words and possibly your favorite word. As we get older, we are taught to be accommodating, to say yes more often than no, and some of us go too far on that path, trying to please everyone except ourselves. Saying no is a powerful way to set boundaries and let people know what you do or do not want. It is important to learn to be comfortable saying no, so those around you can respect your decisions and choices.

Saying *no* is important to me because

_____

_____

_____

_____

_____

_____

_____

_____

_____

_____

⋰ No Does Not Mean Yes ⋱

Below are some examples of ways you can practice saying NO, so you get comfortable using the word NO to set boundaries. There are some more polite ways included for things that need a softer tone, like turning down an invitation to go to the movies. And there are some stronger examples to practice for things that could put you in harm's way. Color the phrases in and then say each one out loud, so you get comfortable asserting yourself. The more you use the word NO, the less it will feel like a bad thing.

"NO THANKS!"

"NOT RIGHT NOW"

"HOW ABOUT ANOTHER TIME?"

"I'M TOO BUSY"

"NO, I DO NOT WANT TO"

"I SAID NO"

"MY ANSWER IS NO"

I CHOOSE
MY THOUGHTS

You have the ability to choose to think positive thoughts or negative thoughts—which do you choose? Most people would pick positive thoughts, of course. But sometimes we can get influenced away from that. Sometimes other people's ideas and thoughts mesh into ours, and we get distracted from what we really feel and think. Learning to choose your own thoughts keeps your voice distinctive, powerful, and yours.

Choosing my thoughts allows me to

_____

_____

_____

_____

_____

_____

_____

_____

_____

_____

I CHOOSE TO BE BRAVE

Being brave can mean anything from speaking your mind to trying something new, like horseback riding or traveling to a new city. It can mean raising your hand in class or befriending the new person at school without asking your other friends whether you should. When we think of bravery, we sometimes think of big things, like a firefighter running into a burning building, but in reality, being brave is usually built with many little moments throughout our day.

The bravest thing I did recently was

_____

_____

_____

_____

_____

_____

_____

_____

_____

I FORGIVE OTHERS

Truly forgiving does not mean that you have to forget, but it *does* mean that you won't continue to punish someone for upsetting or hurting you. Holding on to a grudge damages you and your relationships. You do not have to excuse the behavior or pretend that it didn't hurt you to forgive. Forgiving others in your heart and mind gives you peace and lets you move on in a positive direction.

I was able to forgive _____ **when they**

_____

_____ .

I was able to forgive them by

_____

_____

_____

_____

_____

_____

_____

_____

_____

⌁ Forgiveness Is a Gift ⌁

In the picture below of the gift box, write in people whom you want to forgive. When we genuinely forgive, it is a gift we give to ourselves *and* to others. It lifts a burden from us, and that is an amazing feeling.

I HAVE A
GROWTH MINDSET

Accepting challenges, learning all you can, listening to others' points of view, accepting criticism with an open mind, being happy for others when they succeed—these are all part of having a growth mindset. You accept useful feedback as a way to improve, not as criticism. When you have a growth mindset, you believe that through hard work, listening to others, and some planning, you can achieve whatever you set out to do.

Things I do to help me have a growth mindset are

_____

_____

_____

_____

_____

_____

_____

_____

_____

_____

I LET GO OF WHAT NO LONGER SERVES ME

If something doesn't make you happy, bring you peace, or make your life better, letting go of it is a great gift to yourself. Sometimes we hold on to things—habits, relationships, or physical items—because they once helped us, but they don't any longer. Give yourself permission to walk away from or discard those things that weigh you down and do not still have a positive purpose in your life. This allows you to make space for the good stuff.

The things I will let go of that no longer serve me are

_____

_____

_____

_____

_____

_____

_____

_____

I LOVE MYSELF MORE EACH DAY

Every day you grow and change, which means that every day there are new things to appreciate about yourself. Loving yourself more and more shows that you are progressing in who you want to be. Your potential is endless, and loving yourself adds to that every day.

I tell myself these things to show that I love myself more each day:

_____

_____

_____

_____

_____

_____

_____

_____

_____

_____

_____

I LISTEN TO MY HEART

Listening to your heart means paying attention to feelings you have deep inside. Usually, your first thoughts and instincts about something are right. That immediate response—feeling good or bad about a person or a situation—goes beyond your brain and to the core of your being. When we listen to our heart, we usually cannot go wrong with our decisions.

My heart tells me to

_____

_____

_____

_____

_____

_____

_____

_____

_____

⤜ My Heart Always Knows ⤛

Think about the times in your life when you followed your heart, and it was right. Then write a journal entry detailing those moments, how it felt to listen to your heart, and what happened when you did. Finally, draw a picture of a heart shape in the blank area to remind yourself that your heart is powerful and to listen to it.

_____

_____

_____

_____

_____

_____

_____

_____

_____

_____

_____

_____

_____

_____

_____

I LOVE THE SKIN I AM IN

When you love the skin you're in, you wake up each day being happy about all that is you: your mind, your thoughts, your loves, your body, your decisions. You are content with who you are, what you think, and where you are going. You feel just right being the way you are.

What I love about being in the skin I am in is

_____

_____

_____

_____

_____

_____

_____

_____

_____

_____

_____

I MAKE TIME TO CARE FOR MYSELF

When you make time to care for yourself, you are treating yourself with compassion and respect. Sometimes this means taking a long shower or bubble bath, brushing your hair, and washing your face. Rest and get some good sleep. Feed yourself a meal with good nutrients, get some fresh air, give your body a stretch. These are just some of the ways to take care of yourself. Taking care of yourself is important, because it gives you the energy to tackle whatever comes next in your life.

To take care of my body and my mind, I

_____

_____

_____

_____

_____

_____

_____

_____

_____

I NURTURE MYSELF

Nurturing yourself can include encouraging and supporting your own dreams, giving yourself a break when you need to rest, and eating well so your body feels good. Most of all, it means there is no negative self-talk allowed. Instead, tell yourself that you matter and that whatever you strive for, you can do it!

My favorite nurturing activity is

_____

_____

_____

_____

_____

_____

_____

_____

_____

_____

_____

_____

It is so important to take time for yourself and find clarity. The most important relationship is the one you have with yourself.

—DIANE VON FURSTENBERG,

fashion designer

I PRACTICE SELF-COMPASSION

You are not going to put yourself down. You are going to be as compassionate with yourself as you are with others. You accept that you're not perfect, and you don't criticize yourself for that. When you practice self-compassion, you are putting yourself first on the list of what is important. When we show kindness to ourselves, we have the strength we need to get through difficult times.

I practiced self-compassion when

_____

_____

_____

_____

_____

_____

_____

_____

_____

_____

I PRIORITIZE MYSELF AND MY NEEDS

Putting yourself first is not being selfish. Prioritizing yourself and your needs is an essential step in taking care of your body and mind, getting your work done, and allowing yourself the time you need to rest and recuperate so you can face the next task with even more strength. Prioritizing your needs helps you not feel overwhelmed and out of control. It also lets you gently give boundaries to those around you.

The last time I prioritized myself and my needs I

_____

_____

_____

_____

_____

_____

_____

_____

_____

I RELEASE THE NEED TO JUDGE MYSELF

Self-judging is something most people do. Learning to say no to that behavior is very helpful for your self-esteem. If you can focus on the things you are happy about in your life, and if you can be happy for others for what they have, then the need to judge yourself or compare yourself will vanish. Judging yourself is similar to jealousy: Both are wasted emotions that do not help you strive to do more or be a better person. Instead, find the things you are proud about in yourself and celebrate those!

I no longer judge myself about

_____

_____

_____

_____

_____

_____

_____

I SPEAK WITH KINDNESS

You have choices: you can say something negative, or you can use your words to speak with kindness. Speaking with kindness is what strong, secure people do. They know that putting down others does not make them look better—just the opposite. When we choose to speak with kindness, we show the people around us that we are whole.

I spoke with kindness when I

_____

_____

_____

_____

_____

_____

_____

_____

_____

☼ Positivity Rules ☼

Use the calendar on this page to write in each box one positive thought or action you will strive for every day this month. When we wake up feeling positive, that attitude can carry us through our day with ease.

MONTH _____

1	2	3	4	5
6	7	8	9	10
11	12	13	14	15
16	17	18	19	20
21	22	23	24	25
26	27	28	29	30 / 31

LOVE YOURSELF

This is it—you did it! You completed your journal and have made huge steps along your amazing journey of self-love. Keep practicing the affirmations and lessons you learned in this book to continue growing and blossoming into your awesome, amazing self. Reread your affirmations as much as you want. Consider adding short walks outside or simple meditations to your daily schedule. These are great opportunities to be quiet, listen to your thoughts, and practice what you have learned in this book. And make sure you look in that mirror every day and tell yourself how awesome you are!

RESOURCES

Girls with Confidence. This is an online resource that helps you develop positive self-esteem through workshops and events. GirlsWithConfidence.com.

Just as You Are: A Teen's Guide to Self-Acceptance and Lasting Self-Esteem, by Michelle Skeen and Kelly Skeen. Oakland, CA: Instant Help Books, 2018. This book teaches you how to stop judging yourself and appreciate your unique strengths.

The Ultimate Self-Esteem Workbook for Teens: Overcome Insecurity, Defeat Your Inner Critic, and Live Confidently, by Megan MacCutcheon. Emeryville, CA: Rockridge Press, 2019. This activity book has more than 50 exercises that help you get to know yourself better.

REFERENCES

Common Sense Education. Teens speak out about the benefits and drawbacks of presenting themselves differently (or even anonymously) to others online and consider what it means to "be yourself" in digital spaces. CommonSense.org/education /videos/teen-voices-presenting-yourself-online.

The Girls' Guide to Growth Mindset: A Can-Do Approach to Building Confidence, Courage, and Grit, by Kendra Coates. Emeryville, CA: Rockridge Press, 2020. This is an interactive book to help unlock new adventures, skills, and exploration.

Kids Health. This website has significant sections that help teens with self-esteem. You can choose to read or listen to the programs and ask yourself questions as you go along. KidsHealth.org.

Sit with Us App. This social app was developed by a teenager to encourage inclusive lunchtimes and overall community. SitWithUs.io.

ACKNOWLEDGMENTS

I'd like to thank all the girls and women out there, paving the way and breaking down barriers every day. You are giving the next generation someone to look up to. This is SO important! Much love to my grandmother, who told me that I could do anything the boys did and encouraged me to skateboard, surf, and most important, speak my mind. To my husband, Ian Logan, my biggest supporter of all—I am so lucky to have you cheering me on, no matter what I do next. Huge thanks to my amazing editor, Alyson Penn—I could not have done this without you!

ABOUT THE AUTHOR

 **Cindy Whitehead** (pronouns she/her) is an American professional skateboarder, writer, and activist. Growing up, Cindy was one of the few girls skating half-pipes and pools. At 15 years old, she became the only girl to have a two-page article and centerfold in a skateboarding magazine, where she spoke out about being one of the only girls in a male-dominated sport. She is the author of *It's Not about Pretty: A Book about Radical Skater Girls* and runs the movement Girl Is NOT a 4 Letter Word, which supports and encourages girls to skateboard. Items representing her skateboarding history are part of the Smithsonian National Museum of American History's sports collections in Washington, D.C. Cindy was inducted into the Skateboarding Hall of Fame in 2016 with an introduction by legendary rocker Joan Jett.